DOWN
BUT
NEVER
OUT

Gina Renee Drakeford

Down But Never Out: A Collection of Poetry
By Gina Renee Drakeford

Cover design: Charles Roth
Editor: Laura Daly
Author photo: Christina Altamura

ISBN-13: 978-0-9980454-1-2 (paperback)
ISBN-13: 978-0-9980454-0-5 (e-book)

Poetry

Printed in the United States of America

This book is dedicated to all my loved ones
and to the Care Plus NJ community,
who continue to support my journey.

Contents

Preface

Down But Never Out is meant to be an inspirational book that will give you hope to persevere when inner turmoil is clouding your thoughts. You can read this collection of poetry in any order that speaks to you. The learning experience begins with your being determined to live your life in a manner that's expressed by the title, *Down But Never Out*.

Tragedy struck me in 2001, when I was hit by a car while crossing a street in Teaneck, New Jersey. I remember flying into the air, landing on the hood of the car, sliding down its windshield, then falling on the ground. The doctors at the emergency room where I was taken didn't expect me to survive. That was a life-transforming experience.

After leaving the hospital in a wheelchair, unable to walk, I spent three months at the Kessler Institute for Rehabilitation in East Orange. There I relearned how to move using a walker, then a cane. Today I walk without any assistance. I survived that car accident and am alive and grateful. Yet since the age of 14, nearly three decades before the accident, I've been dealing with mental illness, and there's no cure for that. It's an ongoing disability.

Down But Never Out evolved over the 20 years of hospitalizations that I experienced. Treatment was a revolving door for me. However, my last psychiatric hospitalization was 14 years ago. The reason I have not relapsed is because of my strong faith in God, my higher power, and a vast support network of friends, loved ones, and others who came into my life throughout my journey.

Fourteen years ago I was released from a community hospital with my psychiatrist mandating that I attend a day treatment center five days a week and have home health care aides around the clock. It was either accept those conditions or be sent away to a long-term care facility for many years.

That's when I became a Care Plus New Jersey client in their Partial Care program. Over the years I have received excellent care, and I attribute my success to Care Plus's commitment to helping people with various mental health and other disabilities live full, fulfilling lives.

There's a story behind the way *Down But Never Out* came about. The collection is really written in two parts. Most of the poems in the first half of the book were rewritten from entries in my journal, which I began keeping at age 14. They reflect my initial struggle with mental illness but, more importantly, a shift in mindset that occurred after I participated in the day treatment program at Care Plus New Jersey. Before then I was experiencing writer's block, and my writing seemed rote. But after enrolling in Care Plus New Jersey's weekly journal group and a few years later a poetry and drama group there, I gradually regained my writer's voice, though I still felt frustrated. Then one day I came up with what I now think of as my signature poem, "Down But Never Out," and I've been writing ever since. I eventually became a cofacilitator of the journal group and later the poetry and drama group. I now serve as the volunteer recovery guide in Care Plus New Jersey's Partial Care program. It's rewarding to be able to give back to the organization that helped me.

I am sharing my story with you because for too long mental illness has been presented as something to be ashamed of. It's time for us to acknowledge our illness and work together to help ourselves and others. I hope you will be inspired by this collection. You may gain a new perspective, knowing that you are not alone. You may also discover you have a fighting determination despite whatever issues or problems you're facing. Read it and find a passage or two to help you redirect your thoughts and encourage you to keep pressing on, as I am doing each and every day.

Perseverance

Can You See the Rainbow?

Destitute
Yet viewed as having it
All together
The image presented
To the world:
Self-pride, self-dignity
A warm heart
Genuine concern and compassion
For all humanity

A fragile vessel on the brink
of shattering into pieces
Tiny pieces
Virtually impossible to put back together alone

Once again reaching out for help
Searching for a lifeline to be reeled in

Higher Power
Are you tiring of this constant flow of tears, weariness, doubt
and disbelief?

Look once again
You pour a pitcher of love into a glass and fill it to the brim

What a real thirst quencher

There's a longing for
Strong arms
To openly enfold you

Depression raises its ugly head again
As you drown in a pool of tears you shed

Have you ever been totally deserted?
Sure of experiences of pain
Struggles and disappointments this life brings
Only to make you strong

No matter how endless it may seem, it never lasts

Behind all the tests life presents to you
Your Higher Power never abandons you,
Especially during those times when you are most in need

So
Weep, scream unmercifully
Whatever it takes to release your pent-up emotions
Before you know it,
A rainbow emerges

Blues, Go Away

Blues, go away
You've been here too long
Let me breathe again

The sun wants to shine

Blues, go away
You bring sorrow, rainy days
Sleepless nights

Go away, Blues!

A Change Will Come

What will I do in the morning?
Probably the sun will shine
But in my life, there is sadness
At night my pillow is drenched
With tears of fears and disappointments
A feeling of hopelessness and despair
Colors my nights and days
If I can hold on a little longer
A change will come
A change that will put a smile on my face
And a song in my heart
I'm trusting in my Higher Power
In past times it has always pulled me through
Those low periods of despair
Throughout this life of mine
Many have crossed my path
Guiding me, loving me and directing me
A change has come

Defeated Before Trying

YEAH! Defeated before even trying
Where does your problem lie?
A lack of confidence in yourself
It can be seen through
Your brightest smile
You know you are going to succeed
But
You choose to take the perilous road every time

Continue to Climb

Climb the staircase
Sometimes you will miss a step
Tumbling head first.
Rise, great warrior
Regain your equilibrium
WALK UP THOSE STAIRS
Stumble you shall
Fall you may
But never stop climbing!

Ride First Class

Look inside the dark corners of your mind
There lie answers to your thoughts,
Unsolvable mysteries.
Chase those dreams
Open your eyes to desirable whims.
Don't limit yourself to inflexibility
Spread your wings
Wings longing to take to the sky
Wishing to explore, discover and conquer.

Ride First Class For A Change!

Connections

Come Together as One

Let us all come together as one
The pain we feel
The thoughts we think
The tears we weep
Can be shared together

So that

We can feel each other's pain.
We can wipe away one another's tears.

Let's all come together as one
And only then can we as human beings make it

And come to love the entire human element.

Mankind and the Universe

The world we live in today,
Confusion, disturbances and uncertainty
Surround everyone.

All existing on the brink of
A life of destruction
Confronted by doubt, fear and inner turmoil
Affecting us all on a daily basis.

However, a universal love abides in all of us.

All human beings
Have their own qualities
With the ability to work toward
A brighter tomorrow,
Bringing together all their talents and skills
With a strong desire to spread joy to all
On their journey through this world.

Turning back the clock and beginning anew
Cannot be done
But
Together we will all overcome.

Positive Images

Sun

Peeking out every morning
Gradually brightening
Setting a tone for a new day
Like a flower opening its petals.
Look, the sun is shining brightly
Smiling at all within the universe.
After the warm glow,
The sun sets as it closes its eyes on the world
Yet
Looks forward to shining again
Tomorrow.

Inner Peace

Inner peace
Contentment of mind.
Wonders never cease
Within her
An overabundance
Of love for herself.
Today she grasped it
Slowly opening her eyes
For the first time in her life

BLINDED

By the rays of the sun

Friendship

In its infancy stage
Fascinating new dimensions form.

The newness of the relationship
Dissipates
A volcano may erupt
Why?
A journey is evolving
All eager to explore
The vast complexities of the trip.

Opinions sometimes will differ
Distorting the initial image.

Fun, laughter, tears and anger
Will often manifest themselves.

Although the friendship
All the time is growing and blossoming
Beginning to stand the test of time
Pleasure and consistency are being given
To the friendship that is now almost complete

A new bond is linked
Trust, loyalty, confidentiality and sensitivity manifest
indefinitely
When chosen to dedicate and invest in a true friendship
A bond will form
That will last throughout eternity.

Everlasting Moments of Happiness

Savor each moment of happiness

Digest each delectable morsel.

Store it in a container

For safekeeping.

When it looks as though

Joy has vanished

Remember

Safely tucked away forever

Live

Those treasured moments of

Happiness.

The Hope of Life

Always know that you are not alone on a storm-tossed ocean
Without a life jacket.

I struggle through crises in life
Trying desperately to contact good friends,
Thinking they will see me through this latest storm,
Not realizing while I am in despair
My spiritual source is never far away,
Bringing home to all in the universe.

Sure, it may appear
Sight, touch or other senses should get me through,
But the storm makes it impossible to view life clearly.
It is then that I realize that whatever occurs in life
Is a plan designed for me.

A higher power heals the open wound, broken heart,
Physical illness, mental illness, loss, accident
And all the unplanned events that life brings.

My life jacket is always there to keep me afloat.

Keeping this in mind,
There is no way I cannot win

Transition from Darkness

Down But Never Out

I may be down but never out,
Sure to rise again
And when I do,
I'm coming back fighting
With all the strength
I have within

Storms in Life

Storms in life have a purpose.

Do you ever wonder why
storms are a part of life?

They're unpredictable, unsettling
and usually come without warning.

Storms can bring a myriad of
natural disasters, wind blowing,
Knocking down trees, and floods
that can leave you without all
of your belongings.

Yes, they do come, leaving you
without all those things of
sentimental value.
Those endearing things you held
onto and felt you could never live without.

What's the purpose of a storm?
And how can it change your life
for the better?

That's when your faith
in a power greater than you
kicks in.

There's a reason for every storm,
lessons to be learned
from those unexpected and sometimes
fatal ones too.

Yes, the storms of life will come and go.
Just like change, they are inevitable, you know.
But from each experience you mature
and you grow to lean on
The Most High
You will be encouraged to Trust Yourself
and use the wisdom and discernment
that's inside you at all times.

Persevering, refusing to give up;
You are destined to always pull through.
Look at what you have accomplished,
achieved and, most important,
OVERCOME.

Are you wondering what
your future holds for you?
Don't tarry there too long.

The Most High
The Creator of the Universe
has a unique plan designed
especially for you.

So your pondering
and spending time wondering,
"What are my gifts and talents?
And what will my contribution
to this life be?"

Stop

Do not spend another second
of your precious time contemplating
whatever your gifts and talents

may or may not be.

Rest assured
You do have them.
Yes, they do exist.
And you bring your
very unique and special qualities.

The Almighty's plan for you
may differ from what you believe
to be true.

Hold on to your faith and
let hope lead the way.

Think positively and believe
what's ultimately destined
for you in this life will be

AWESOME!

And it will manifest itself in due time
And in a MIRACULOUS WAY TOO!

What Will This Day Bring?

I woke up this morning wondering
What will this day bring?
Will it bring happiness?
Will it bring sadness?

Then ...

Once again I wondered
What will this day bring?
Will I succumb?

Or ...

Will I take charge?
And if yes,
How will I handle it?
To my surprise
I caught the ball,

Ran with it

And made a touchdown.

Today the sun is shining

And

Life is not controlling me

I'm taking charge of it.

Insight through Self-Reflection

Are You Expecting a Reawakening of Life?

Let's stop for a moment and regroup.
Life has its ups and downs

Yet one must reflect on the positive.
Negativity will only drag you down.

You will find yourself living
more of a zestful life.

Stretch your arms out to your Higher Power and focus on
those issues that need your guidance and direction.

It may seem as though you're not getting anywhere.

However, keep making strides
Because your Creator will always protect you from your
self-destruction.

Listen, it's time for you to let go of
those unwarranted thoughts

STEP OUT ON FAITH!

Dismiss being solely a survivor.
Grasp onto taking baby steps,
And before you realize it,
You will find yourself THRIVING

NOW YOU ARE LIVING
A REAWAKENING OF LIFE

Anybody Can Quit

It's so easy to give up and quit
The real test in life is
Taking all that you have been provided with,
Determination,
Courage and willpower,
Just
To name a few.

Then take your
Free will to choose
And
Decide to find your way back
To that fighting spirit of yours,
Reclaim your willingness
To challenge yourself
To live.
Take hold of the reins,
Like riding a horse
Now
Use all your gifts and talents
To help others
Who too are struggling
With a desire to give up
And quit.

Hope you have come to the
Realization
You have the fortitude to

Persevere

First take the focus off
Yourself.
Help out wherever you can
Then
Strive to be an example to
Your fellow man.

Anybody Can Change

Anybody can change
How, why and when
Are the major pieces
Of the puzzle.

Can anybody change?
Yes, yet there are various
Schools of thought.
To begin with, take the mind
What a powerful part of one's psyche.
It is like a sponge absorbing
Whatever thoughts that filter in.

Anybody can change
It's a process, a lifelong one.
Your view of your life
Ultimately plays a major role
Particularly whether or not
You believe you can change
Or
if you would like to change.

Spiritually, many believe there's
A power greater than them
And that Spiritual Source
Has the power to
Change anybody.
Like the way it breathes

Life into the very soul of every living individual.

Many people
Wake up every morning
Thankful and grateful to
Be able to move and have their faculties.

This carries them through.

Anybody can change
Being grounded in
Faith and Hope
And confident
That brighter days are yet to
Come around for them.

Anybody can change

When you have that strong, determined
Belief of Something of Great Magnitude
You can hold on to and go to for help.

Whatever that Source is for you
And it's worked successfully
Throughout your life
Disregard whatever others may say
Who try to discredit you.
You have reached the mountaintop

Yes
Anybody can change.

Turning The Corner

Do Not Delay

Do Not Delay
Time passes moment by moment
That's how it is meant to be.
It leaves no time for dwelling on
Past regrets that cannot be changed.

Do Not Delay
Live in the moment,
Each moment of each day.
Capture that beautiful butterfly
On this bright sunny day.

Do Not Delay
Butterflies move fast.
You do not want to get
Distracted and miss out
On the beauty of nature:

Get out of your own way.
Stop dwelling on the things
You have no control over.

Do Not Delay
Because if you do
You will miss out on
The awesome plan
The Creator has designed for you and only you

Little Red Wagon

Everybody has their own Little Red Wagon to pull.

Each day you awaken
You are faced with
Your own Little Red Wagon to pull

It's there to teach you
Life's lessons along the way.

You may be wondering,
What is in the
Little Red Wagon?

Its contents are unique
And vary from person to person.

Yet
We all have our own
Little Red Wagon to pull
At times it's heavier than others.

There are times when your
Little Red Wagon will pull you down too.
Finding yourself falling
Without a warning or a clue.

Keep in mind
The Creator of the Universe is always walking alongside you,
providing strength
And giving you all you need to pick yourself up.

Ask For Help.

To your surprise

Already within you lives

The courage and strength
To put all your cares and all your troubles aside,
Right back in your Little Red Wagon,
You and your determination will start pulling it again.

The ultimate message:
Everybody has their own Little Red Wagon to pull
It's there to inspire you and encourage you to
Have faith and trust in all that you do.

Where Do You Go from Here?

Venture out of your comfort zone.
Decide this moment to let go
And meet new challenges head on.

This is a new territory
For you to explore.
When you stop for a moment
And think about this approach

What is there to lose?
Out with the old way of doing things
And discover a whole new world

Skepticism and a bundle of nerves
You may be experiencing now
But trying something new
Often leads to opportunities

Also, a learning experience
Has its ups and downs
However, little do you know

The Almighty is preparing you
To be ready to handle
The ultimate plan
Designed just for you.

Let go of the old

Be bold
Be courageous
Try a new and different way
You may end up surprised
At all the knowledge you've gained
And the life experience attained.

Light

Shines Forth

Where Do You Find Inspiration?

Inspiration
Where can inspiration be found?
When life tests you
With challenges and you're faced
With adversity

Friends and acquaintances
You may often seek out;
But finding inspiration from man
Can be tricky

Often judgment is passed and
Then one may become
Confused

But where do you find inspiration?
You try searching within your soul
Sometimes answers can be found

But inspiration always can be
Found in a power greater
Than yourself

It's that source that motivates
You to wake up and face another day

I find most inspiration
When I fall down on my knees
And cry out to the Most High for help
My source of strength

After learning and focusing only on the Almighty
My poetry flows,

Life arrives when writing,
My heart sings out with joy

I've found that when I let go
And let the Creator shine through
Inspiration can be found in all
That I encounter along the way
As I sojourn on this earth

What a Wonderful Way to Welcome in a Brand-New Day

What a wonderful way
To welcome in
A brand-new day

Woke up this morning,
Not a cloud in sight.
The warmth of the sun
Has me feeling
Free of anger
Free of anxiety
Free of self-doubt.

Clearly
It's a great way
To start the day.
In celebration of
The positive energy
That is felt throughout,
Decided today
Words of encouragement
Will be the way
To bring a glimmer of hope
To others who are struggling
To find their way.

A smile, a kind word
May soothe their soul,
Leaving them feeling
Cared about
And made to feel whole.

 Tribute

You All Know Who You Are

Yes, You All Know Who You Are
The special and endearing ones
Who positively impact my life.
You individually and collectively
Contribute to my becoming whole.

You All Know Who You Are

Often through my prose and poetry,
I share a glimpse of my life with you,
Which indicates the direction
It is now moving in.

You All Know Who You Are

At this very moment
I feel compelled to express
The words: Thank You. Also,
Please allow me to extend
My heartfelt gratitude and appreciation.

You All Know Who You Are

Positive feedback, constructive criticism,
Attentive and astute listeners show
How genuine and interested
You are in my well-being.

This is why another moment
In our lives I dare not let go by
Without my giving you all
Your flowers while you are still
      Alive.

Spiritually, I am blessed by
The Most High, who has placed
Me in your hands to encourage me,
To inspire me to persevere,
Despite what unexpected trials
Try to play havoc with my mind.
      Yet
I am not to be prideful but to
Humble myself. And
I am to help others along the way
Who like me are striving to make
A difference in this Journey we
All are traveling.

AGAIN, I EXTEND MY APPRECIATION
      AND
      MY GRATITUDE TO YOU

YOU ALL KNOW WHO YOU ARE

Made in the USA
Monee, IL
04 May 2021

67618410R00032